My First BIG Read With Me Book

Written by Helen Jones

First published 2020 by Brown Watson
The Old Mill, 76 Fleckney Road
Kibworth Beauchamp
Leicestershire LE8 0HG

ISBN: 978-0-7097-2799-6
© 2020 Brown Watson, England
Printed in Malaysia

Brown Watson
ENGLAND

Contents

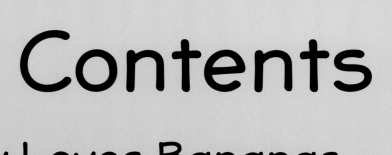

Dinky Loves Bananas

Giraffe was the tallest animal at Sunnydale Safari Park. But that was about to change when Ostrich found a strange egg in her nest. "That's not mine!" she said. "How did that get there?" But no one knew.

The next day the egg started to crack. "Come and see!" Ostrich called the others. Out popped a little head. Then a very long neck and finally the funniest creature you ever saw. "What is it?" asked Lion. But no one knew.

Ostrich was delighted. "I'm going to call her Dinky!" she said. Dinky sniffed the air. "Are you hungry?" asked Ostrich. "Leaves?" offered Giraffe. "Meat?" said Lion. But Dinky shook her head furiously. "Bananas!" she said.

"Her first word!" cooed Ostrich. "But what does it mean?" said Giraffe. "I think we're about to find out," said Lion. "BANANAS!" cried Dinky and bounded off. The animals chased after her. But Dinky was fast. She was heading for the monkeys' hideout.

"Looks like she's found what she was after," said Lion as they watched her eat the monkeys' bananas. From then on, Dinky ate bananas, until one day... "Sorry, Dinky," said Big Monkey. "We're all out of bananas. You'll have to find your own supply."

Dinky slowly walked back to her friends. As she did so, something amazing happened... She grew... and grew... and GREW!

"Look at Dinky!" cried Lion. "She's even taller than Giraffe."

"So she is," said Ostrich. "But at least now she can reach her own bananas!"

CAN YOU FIND THESE PICTURES?

lion

eggs

tree

monkey

rock

grasshopper

CAN YOU FIND THESE WORDS?

safari park

ostrich

lion

giraffe

creature

bananas

leaves

meat

egg

walked

friends

animals

nest

monkey

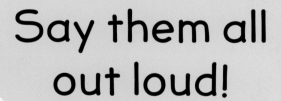

Say them all
out loud!

When I Grow Up

Laura loved going to the museum with her mum. "How many bones does this dinosaur have?" she asked the curator. "What did it eat? How long did it live for?" "That's a lot of questions," he laughed. "I want to be a scientist when I grow up," Laura explained.

In the afternoon Laura played outside with her friends. "You're really fast on roller skates," said Sarah. "And you can spin," said Mark. "Well…" said Laura. "I'd like to be an athlete when I grow up." "Time for ballet, Laura!" called Mum.

Laura loved her ballet class. She pointed her toes, jumped up and down and twirled around. "Well done!" said Mrs Thomas. "I'm going to be a ballet dancer when I grow up," said Laura, "and go on a big stage."

"Would you like a milkshake now?" asked Mum when they got home. "Yes, please," said Laura. "Can I have banana... chocolate... and strawberry?" Laura loved choosing the ingredients. "I think I'd like to be a chef when I grow up," she said.

"Brush your teeth before bedtime," said Mum. While Laura was brushing her teeth she showed Teddy how to do it. "Don't miss the back ones," she said. "You'll be telling us you want to be a dentist next!" laughed Mum.

"I hear you want to be a scientist... chef... ballet dancer or athlete," said Dad. "I can't decide which," said Laura. "There's plenty of time for that," laughed Dad. "Well in any case," said Laura, snuggling up to him, "I hope I'll be as clever as you."

CAN YOU FIND THESE PICTURES?

helmet

roller skates

teddy

book

mixer

radio

CAN YOU FIND THESE WORDS?

museum

scientist

chef

ballet dancer

athlete

banana

chocolate

strawberry

milkshake

decide

teeth

dentist

teddy

ingredients

Say them all out loud!

Storm at Sea!

"Hold on tight!" shouted Captain Kipper as a massive wave crashed over the boat, drenching the sailors...

The next morning the storm was over but the ship was a mess. "We've lost everything!" sighed Captain Kipper. "And the ship is badly damaged."

"Don't worry," said Percy. "Perhaps we can catch a few fish. And I'll keep a lookout for land." Suddenly Percy spotted a mermaid in the water. She cried out to him, "Help! Help!"

"My tail is caught!" she cried. "Quick!" Percy said to the crew. "Get your swords and cut through this netting!" They set to work and soon the mermaid was able to swim freely again. "Thank you!" she said. "How can I ever reward you?"

Just then she had an idea. "Can any of you dive?" she asked. "We can," said Percy and Oliver. "Well, then. Come with me!" said the mermaid. Oliver and Percy put on their diving suits and followed the mermaid down to the seabed. "A shipwreck!" gasped Percy.

"And look at that treasure chest!" said Oliver, excitedly. "Can you open it?" said the mermaid. "I've tried. But I'm not strong enough." Percy and Oliver prised the lid open and inside were hundreds of gold coins! "Wow! More than enough to fix the boat," said Oliver.

Everyone helped to haul the treasure chest out of the water. "Well done, lads!" said Captain Kipper. "We'll be feasting tonight!"

"I fancy a nice juicy steak," said Percy. "And I'd like chocolate pudding," said Oliver. "Land ahoy!" cried the cabin boy and everyone cheered.

CAN YOU FIND THESE PICTURES?

treasure chest

coral

seagull

fish

sword

coins

CAN YOU FIND THESE WORDS?

mermaid

treasure chest

chocolate pudding

steak

ship

diving suit

swim

swords

gold coins

sailors

shipwreck

seabed

netting

Say them all out loud!

Daniel's Pet

Daniel was a bit shy and didn't have many friends at school. Sometimes at playtime he would make friends with the little creatures in the long grass. He knew everything about them – how many wings they had, what they ate and where they slept.

Today it was bring-a-pet day at Daniel's school. "Now… we've seen Sammy's snake and Rebecca's rabbit," said Mrs Field. "What have you brought to show us Daniel?"
Daniel went to the front and hoped the children wouldn't laugh at his pet.

Daniel opened the lid of a shoebox and inside was a baby dragon. "Ooh!" gasped the children. "Is he dangerous?" asked Brenda. "No," said Daniel. "He's just a bit naughty sometimes." Suddenly the dragon stretched its wings and flew around the classroom.

The dragon promptly ate the houseplant, a shoelace and the whole of Daniel's packed lunch! "Oh dear!" said Mrs Field. "What shall we do?" But Daniel knew what to do. He gave a special whistle and immediately the dragon flew back into his box!

That afternoon in the playground, all the children swarmed around Daniel. "Where does your dragon come from?" they asked. "Does he breathe fire?" Despite his shyness Daniel enjoyed telling them all about his dragon.

Suddenly a voice shouted, "Come and see this llama, everybody!" The children ran off, apart from one little girl. "I've got a pet dragon, too," she told Daniel. "Would you like to see him sometime?" "I'd love to," he said. He had a feeling he'd made a new friend.

CAN YOU FIND THESE PICTURES?

poster

clock

slide

plant

butterfly

spider

CAN YOU FIND THESE WORDS?

children
shy
rabbit
snake
shoebox
dragon
llama

playground
creatures
girl
houseplant
lunch
shoelace
classroom

Say them all out loud!

Rusty and Scrap's Adventure

Rusty and Scrap lived in an unlocked garage. "I don't get out much these days," said Rusty. "Me neither," sighed Scrap. Suddenly they heard the sound of footsteps running towards them. "We're in luck, Sid," said a voice and the garage door opened.

Two robbers stepped inside. "What have we here, Larry?"

"A rusty old car and a clapped out truck." "I'm a campervan," said Scrap. "Not a truck." Just then they heard a police siren. "Quick," said Larry. "Let's take both of them."

"Can't you go any faster than this?"
growled Larry. "I'm doing my best,"
snapped Rusty.

"Useless truck," said Sid. "Do you mind,"
said Scrap. "I'm a campervan!"

But despite the tension, Rusty and
Scrap were secretly thrilled to be
having an adventure again.

Suddenly Rusty's engine started to splutter and he came to a stop. And Scrap got a puncture and stood still too. "AARRGGHH!" said the robbers as the police car pulled up alongside them. "OK," said one policeman. "Game's over boys! Hand over the money."

The policeman took a look at Rusty and Scrap. "Just as well you two are a bit... ahem... slow!" he said. "You saved the day!" "Mind you," said the policeman scratching his head. "I wonder..."

Some weeks later... Rusty and Scrap met up again. "The policeman did me up and sold me on to a lovely couple," said Rusty. "And he decided to keep me for family holidays," said Scrap. "Fancy a race?" "Why not?" said Rusty.

CAN YOU FIND THESE PICTURES?

seagull

police

car

robber

boat

police hat

CAN YOU FIND THESE WORDS?

campervan

car

policeman

engine

puncture

robbers

police car

couple

garage

truck

siren

money

holidays

rusty

Say them all out loud!

Sukie in Space

"Three... two... one... BLAST OFF! "
Where are we off to today?" asked
Mandy, once the rocket was safely
heading into space. "Planet Fiddlesticks,"
said Jake. "Space School have asked us
to do some scientific research there."
"Great!" said Mandy.

"Shh!" said Jake suddenly. "What's that noise?" They both listened carefully.
"It sounds like ... a cat!" said Jake.
"Sukie! How on earth did you get here?"
"Oh dear!" said Mandy. "She must have slipped in without us noticing."

Mandy and Jake landed on Planet
Fiddlesticks and started looking at the
rocks. Sukie thought rocks were boring
so she found some funny friends to play
with instead. "Sukie! Sukie!"
Mandy called. "Ah there you are.
Time to go home, now."

They were heading for Earth when suddenly the warning light started flashing. "Uh-oh!" said Jake. "There's a leak in the fuel tank. I think I can fix it... if only we had something to plug in the hole."

"Let's look for anything that might work."

"How about using Sukie's bell?" said Mandy. "Good idea! So... the chewing gum can stick the bell in place then we'll tie the sock here like this... HURRAY! It works!" But their joy was short-lived. Beep! Beep! Beep! "We're nearly out of fuel. Will we make it back?"

That afternoon at Space School, the head teacher made an announcement. "Please give a big round of applause to Jake and Mandy. Today they showed great bravery and resourcefulness on their space flight. Oh, and I believe Sukie the cat also played her part. Well done!" Everyone cheered.

CAN YOU FIND THESE PICTURES?

alien

flying saucer

teacher

map

stars

earth

CAN YOU FIND THESE WORDS?

chewing gum

bell

bravery

leak

fuel

rocket

hole

space

rocks

warning light

flight

Sukie the cat

round of applause

funny friends

Say them all out loud!

The School Fair

"There's going to be a summer fair," said Jade on the way home from school. "Mrs Price told us there would even be a big wheel. And we can wear fancy dress. Can I go as a princess please, Mum?"

"I'll see what I can do," said Mum.

The day of the fair arrived. Jade's Mum was baking some cakes for the stall. "I'll help," said Jade. Soon there was a lovely smell of chocolate cake coming from the kitchen. "Hey! Get out, Sammy," Mum told the dog. "These aren't for you!"

"Thanks for helping, Jade," said Mum once they had set up the cake stall. "Go and enjoy the fair with your friend Annabel." Jade was very excited. There was so much to see – craft stalls, hat stalls, jugglers, clowns and a puppet show.

Jade's friend Peter was dressed as a knight. But he couldn't see where he was going and bumped into Ollie. "NO!" said Ollie. "I've got orange juice all down my costume now. Hrrumph!" And he stormed off. "Now I know why he chose that outfit," said Jade giggling.

"Come on!" said Annabel. "Let's go on the big wheel." Jade had never been up so high. Everyone looked so tiny below her. Just then she spotted a long queue of people at Mum's stall. "Hi, Mum!" she waved.

"That was fun," said Annabel. "Are you staying for the fireworks?" "Fireworks! Wow!" said Jade. "Let's go and ask my mum – race you!" Mum had sold all the cakes. "I hear there are fireworks," she said. "Shall we stay and watch?" "Yes please!" said Jade.

CAN YOU FIND THESE PICTURES?

firework

puppy

ogre

knight

hats

cake

CAN YOU FIND THESE WORDS?

fair

princess

fancy dress

kitchen

wardrobe

cakes

hat stall

jugglers

clowns

knight

ogre

orange juice

big wheel

fireworks

Say them all out loud!

CAN YOU FIND THESE WORDS?

giraffe
found
mine
others
funniest
asked
supply

grew
curator
laughed
athlete
ballet
big
grow

teddy

tellling

snuggling

clever

drenching

storm

badly

cried

reward

seabed

creatures

friends

ate

slept

brought

breathe

feeling

voice

quick

fancy

CAN YOU FIND THESE PICTURES?

giraffe

caterpillar

mermaid

teacher

cat

dino egg

bones

pirate

dragon

sandwiches

knight

cupcakes

Goodbye!